Angry Mom Loves Me Too

Mama me voli i kad je ljuta

Mati me ima rada i kad je huda

Marija Brezak

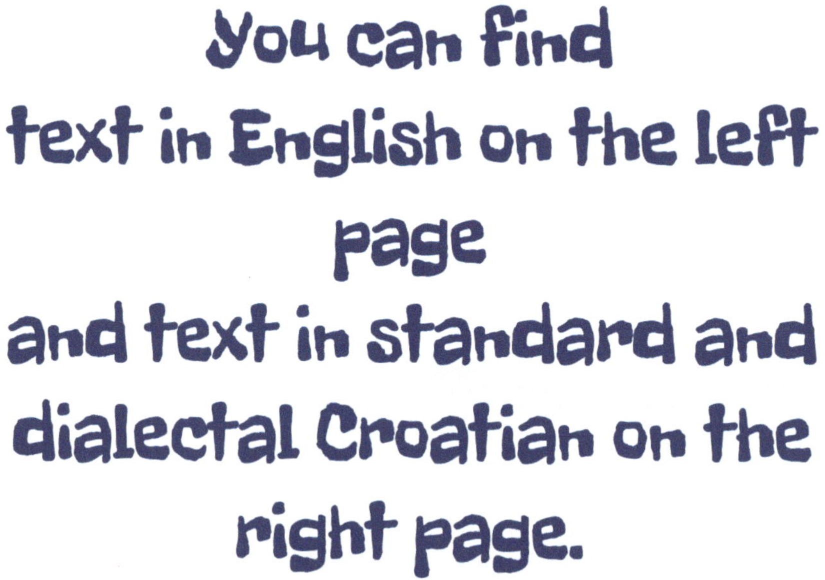

Copyedited by Martina Tomorad (English)
Copyedited by Željka Meštrović Kruhak (Croatian)

CROATIA
HRVATSKA

Na svakoj stranici možete pronaći tekst na engleskome jeziku na lijevoj strani i tekst na standardnome hrvatskome jeziku i kajkavskome narječju na desnoj strani.

LOCATION OF THE DIALETCT IN CROATIA
TU SME I KAJ NAM PAK MOREJU!?

Na sake strane morete najti tekst na engleski na lijeve strane i tekst na štokavski i po domaći na desne strane.

There's a place to write and draw and put photos at the end of the book!
Na kraju knjige imate mjesto za fotografije, poruke i crteže!

To all the moms out there that sometimes "lose it" - you are not alone.

To all the children out there that help us find our way - thank you for your pure existence.

Svim majkama koje ponekad izgube živce - niste same. Svoj djeci koja nam pomognu vratiti se na pravi put - hvala vam što postojite!

Sem materami tere negda prehiti - nijeste same. Se dece tera nas zdigneju nazaj - fala vam koj nas bavite.

I can feel your little
kicks.
Can you hear my heart?
I wrapped my arms
around you
from the very
start.

Osjećala sam tvoje lupkanje!
Sjećaš li se zvuka srca moga?
Od samog početka sam strepila
i čekala osmijeh lica tvoga.

Osetila sam kak me ječeš.
E se čule kak ti popijevam?
Od navek te gladim, čuvam i branim
i stiha ruke na te dijevam.

Are you surprised?
Believe me, it´s true!
When I was
pregnant,
I have already loved
you.

Čudiš li se tome?
Misliš da je šala?
Već tada sam te voljela,
bubice moja mala.

Možda te fejst to čudi,
al' od rana sam rad te imijela.
Dok te još nisam dijela pod perut,
v srce sam svoje tebe prijela.

I have showed you how to walk,
how to eat and how to talk.

Odmah sam ti pokazala
kako možeš fino jesti,
kako trebaš puno pričati,
brzo hodati pa na guzu sjesti.

Zaranam sam ti pokazala
kak se ravne hodi,
kak se štučne jede
kak se pune govori.
i kak se pune govori.

But the most important thing
I want you to know,
is how to really love,
so you could fully grow.

Pružala sam pravu ljubav
kako najbolje sam znala.
Tražila sam je u sebi
da bih ti je dala.

Al' od sega mi je bitneše
da pravu ljubav dobiš.
Da mi fejst narasteš
i okole ju deliš.

You can be angry,
you can be loud.
Just don't break or hit
and I will be proud.

Ljubav podnosi ljutnju,
vikanje i buku,
no ljudi koji vole
ne lome i ne tuku.

Moreš se jake srditi,
moreš kričati i noriti.
Same te lijepe prosim
naj niš hitati i druge biti.

Always
remember –
my love is true!
Even when I´m
loud,
I still love you.

Ti zauvijek pamti -
tu prava ljubav vlada.
Ponekad sam glasna,
no volim te i tada.

Zanavek pamti -
med nami prava ljubav vlada.
I onda kad jake zijam,
fejst te imam rada.

Sometimes I'm angry.
Sometimes I'm upset.
But do I still love you?
Yes, you bet!

Ima dana kad poludim.
Ima dana kad sam ljuta.
Volim li te čak i tada?
Duplo više i još sto puta!

I ja sam negda huda.
I ja sam negda srdita.
Al' pod sim tim bijesem,
velika ljubav je skrita.

Always
remember -
my love is true!
Even when I´m
angry,
I still love you.

Ti zauvijek pamti –
tu prava ljubav vlada.
Ponekad sam ljuta,
no volim te i tada.

Navijek se zmisli –
med nami prava ljubav vlada.
I kad sam jake huda,
fejst te imam rada.

You know those days
when I look
like a bat?

When I'm
hungry
or tired
I sometimes
get upset.

Znaš li one dane
kad šišmišu sličim?
Opasna sam kad sam gladna –
time se ne dičim.

Znaš da ima dani
kad ausvinklin zgledam.
Ak sam lačna i pospana,
primiriti se ne dam.

Always remember -
my love is true!
Even when I´m upset,
I still love you.

Ti zauvijek pamti –
tu prava ljubav vlada.
Ponekad sam nervozna,
no volim te i tada.

Nigdar ne pozabi –
med nami prava ljubav vlada.
I kad sam jake nora,
fejst te imam rada.

Don't you worry!
Moms can look blue,
or even a bit crazy,
but still love you!

I onih dana ima
kada sam ti čudna,
kada puno plačem
u snu i budna.

Već pomalu vidiš –
mame moreju naopak biti.
Moreju biti fejst vesele,
Moreju biti fejst vesele,
a sejene suzu pustiti.

Always remember -
my love is true!
Even when I´m sad,
I still love you.

Ti zauvijek pamti –
tu prava ljubav vlada.
Ponekad sam tužna,
no volim te i tada.

Zanavek pamti –
med nami prava ljubav vlada.
I kad se jake plačem,
fejst te imam rada.

Let's make some coffee!
I need my fuel.
Life without sleep is so cruel.

Za prvu mi pomoć
tu je uvijek kava.
Svakome je teško
kad noću ne spava.

Ideme skuhati kavu.
Bez toga teške mižem.
Već duge slabe spim
i tak se teške dižem.

Always
remember -
my love is true!
Even when I'm
tired,
I still love you.

Ti zauvijek pamti -
tu prava ljubav vlada.
Ponekad sam umorna,
no volim te i tada.

Navijek se zmisli -
med nami prava ljubav vlada.
I kad sam ko pes umorna,
fejst te imam rada.

And in the evening when you won't go
to bed, I am so sleepy
I might turn mad.
HA
HA

Najteže je noću
kad ne želiš leći.
Beskrajno sam umorna
pa bijes postaje veći.

A kad mi se navečer
ne daš v krevet deti,
ja si točne mislim
da bi mogla ponoreti.

Always
remember -
my love is true!
Even when I´m
mad,
I still love you.

Ti zauvijek pamti -
tu prava ljubav vlada.
Ponekad sam bijesna,
no volim te i tada.

Nigdar ne pozabi -
med nami prava ljubav vlada.
I kad do kraja ponorim,
fejst te imam rada.

Please don't
scream,
be a doll.
I'm so tired
I could fall.

Molim te ne viči
baš ovako jako.
Tako sam pospana
da past ću lako.

Prosim te, naj kričati.
Bez vuh bum ostala.
Joj kak jake zijaš.
Na pleča bum opala!

Always remember -
my love is true!
Even when you
scream,
I still love you.

Zauvijek pamti -
tu prava ljubav vlada.
Ponekad se dereš,
no volim te i tada.

Bez brige mi budi,
med nami prava ljubav vlada.
I kad jake kričiš
fejst te imam rada.

We can feel anger,
but love is still there.
Feel free to be angry.
My love can bear!

Slobodno se ljuti.
Ne drži to u sebi!
Bijes trebaš pustiti
da preplavio te ne bi.

I onda kad nekoga jake voliš,
moreš na njega srdit biti.
Kak se srditi, a ne nikoga gnjesti?
E, to je negda teške nafčiti.

Just let it all out!
My arms are open
wide.
I am waiting for you
if you need a place
to hide.

Ja ne želim biti vatra,
a ni voda bijesu tvome.
Ja sam samo mirna luka.
Nađi mir u krilu mome.

Same se fajn znori
i se to pusti proč.
Ja sam ovde za te
baš saki dan i noć.

I will always love you
no matter what life brings.
I'm here to support you,
so you could spread your wings.

I kad je sunce visoko na nebu,
i kad su magle crne i guste,
majke pružaju svoje ruke
koje vas drže, ali i puste.

Ti si moj mali tiček.
Ja splela sam za te gnijezde.
Al' nije ti meste pri drijevu -
poleti i primi se zvijezde.

Our roots are tangled together
not to hold you tight,
but to give you strength
and a strong loving heart.

Naše su niti prepletene
u divnoj čaroliji života.
Neka ti daju sidro i snagu.
Neka te vode ljubav i dobrota

Nek one te vodiju kam god letiš.
Ja sam vu srcu ti blizu navijek.
Nek su ti puti vu sreće i smijehu,
a doma te čeka ljubavi cijeli brijeg.

I asked my mom why she loves me and she said...

Mama zašto me voliš?

DATE:

My mom asked me why I love her and I said...

Mama volim te jer...

DATE:

OUR FAMILY

YOU'RE SO CUTE!
CUTE
Photobooth
So proud of you
Photobooth

THIS IS:

DATE:

THIS IS:

DATE:

THIS IS:

DATE:

THIS IS:

DATE:

Marija Brezak was born and raised in Croatia. As a speech-language therapist, she writes and illustrates for her little clients daily. This is her first picture book, written as a birthday present for her children. She loves nature, gardening and growing vegetables, spending time in the forest, singing, playing the guitar and the trumpet. She has a husband and two beautiful children that inspire her.

Marija Brezak je rođena i odrasla u Hrvatskoj. Kao logopetkinja svakodnevno piše i crta za svoje male korisnike. Ovo je njezina prva slikovnica napisana kao rođendanski poklon njezinoj djeci. Voli vrtlariti i uzgajati povrće, provoditi vrijeme u šumi, pjevati te svirati gitaru i trubu. Ima muža i dvoje djece koji su joj neiscrpna inspiracija.

www.ingramcontent.com/pod-product-compliance
Lightning Source LLC
LaVergne TN
LVHW071139160826
845679LV00027B/1163
9798355348816